This Prayer Journal Belongs To:

_____

Roma Waterman 2022

All materials contained in this book are the copyrighted property of Roma Waterman trading as I Was Carried Pty Ltd. To reproduce, republish, post, modify, distribute or display material from this publication, you must first obtain permission for the author at:

Roma Waterman
P O Box 288
Warrandyte, Victoria
Melbourne, Australia 3113

roma@romawaterman.com
www.romawaterman.com
training.romawaterman.com
Published by: I Was Carried Pty Ltd
Distributed by: I Was Carried Pty Ltd

ISBN: 978-0-646-86152-4

Writing, Editing & Design by Roma Waterman
Formatting and pre-press by Joshua Halls at Roar Kingdom Creative
Printed in Australia

Hey Friend,

I'm so glad you are here! If you have picked up this journal it is because you love to pray, or you want to pray more intentionally.

If you are like me, you have been pondering all that is going on in the world right now....and it is making you want to cling to Jesus more than ever. I am convinced that the only way we can truly understand, know, and see Him being revealed powerfully in our lives is simple.... PRAY!

Prayer creates a common union between us and God. It is the common thread that weaves His purposes and plants into the very fabric of our lives. It is what holds everything together.

I pray this journal creates more intentional moments of powerful prayers in your day. It has been kept simple intentionally. You can begin with a SCRIPTURE that you feel the Lord is leading you to, then begin by listing some of your prayer requests in the PRAYER section. This is followed by a DEVOTIONAL section to share your thoughts on the scripture for the day. Then there is ANSWERED PRAYERS to record any prayers that were answered, followed by I AM THANKFUL FOR, PRAYING FOR OTHERS and finally, NOTES AND REFLECTION, should you have more in your heart to write down.

You can use this journal daily or weekly. The joy of being more intentional is you can look back through your journal and see how the Lord has been speaking to you, and how faithful He will be in answering your heartfelt prayers.

Be blessed as you reach out to Him today,

Roma Waterman

I can do all this through Him who gives me strength.

———————

Philippians 4:13

Prayer Journal

Scriptures To Live by

This is the confidence we have in approaching God: that if we ask anything according to his will, he hears us. 1 John 5:14

And if we know that he hears us—whatever we ask—we know that we have what we asked of him. 1 John 5:15

Therefore I tell you, whatever you ask for in prayer, believe that you have received it, and it will be yours. Mark 11:24

Do not be anxious about anything, but in every situation, by prayer and petition, with thanksgiving, present your requests to God. And the peace of God, which transcends all understanding, will guard your hearts and your minds in Christ Jesus. Philippians 4:6-7

Look to the LORD and his strength; seek his face always. 1 Chronicles 16:11

If my people, who are called by my name, will humble themselves and pray and seek my face and turn from their wicked ways, then I will hear from heaven, and I will forgive their sin and will heal their land.
1 Chronicles 7:14

I pray that the eyes of your heart may be enlightened in order that you may know the hope to which he has called you, the riches of his glorious inheritance in his holy people. Ephesians 1:18

And pray in the Spirit on all occasions with all kinds of prayers and requests. With this in mind, be alert and always keep on praying for all the Lord's people. Ephesians 6:18

The LORD detests the sacrifice of the wicked, but the prayer of the upright pleases him. Proverbs 15:8

Prayer Journal

Date:

Today's Passage:

_____

Prayer:
_____
_____
_____
_____
_____

Devotional:
_____
_____
_____
_____
_____

My Prayers that were Answered:
_____
_____
_____
_____
_____

I am Thankful for:
_____
_____
_____
_____
_____

My Prayers for Others:
_____
_____
_____
_____
_____
_____
_____

Notes and Reflections:
_____
_____
_____
_____
_____
_____
_____
_____
_____
_____
_____
_____
_____
_____
_____

I trust the next chapter because I know the author.

Finally, be strong in the Lord and in the strength of his might.

───────────

Ephesians 6:10

Prayer Journal

Date:

Today's Passage:

_____

Prayer:
_____
_____
_____
_____
_____

Devotional:
_____
_____
_____
_____
_____

My Prayers that were Answered:
_____
_____
_____
_____
_____

I am Thankful for:
_____
_____
_____
_____
_____

My Prayers for Others:

_____
_____
_____
_____
_____
_____
_____
_____

Notes and Reflections:

_____
_____
_____
_____
_____
_____
_____
_____
_____
_____
_____
_____
_____
_____
_____
_____
_____

Prayer Journal

Date:

Today's Passage:

_____

Prayer:
_____
_____
_____
_____

Devotional:
_____
_____
_____
_____

My Prayers that were Answered:
_____
_____
_____
_____

I am Thankful for:
_____
_____
_____
_____

My Prayers for Others:

___

Notes and Reflections:

___

Prayer Journal

Date:

Today's Passage:

Prayer:
_____
_____
_____
_____
_____

Devotional:
_____
_____
_____
_____
_____

My Prayers that were Answered:
_____
_____
_____
_____
_____

I am Thankful for:
_____
_____
_____
_____
_____

My Prayers for Others:
___
___
___
___
___
___
___
___
___

Notes and Reflections:
___
___
___
___
___
___
___
___
___
___
___
___
___
___
___
___
___
___
___

Prayer Journal

Date:

Today's Passage:

_____

Prayer:

_____
_____
_____
_____
_____

Devotional:

_____
_____
_____
_____
_____

My Prayers that were Answered:

_____
_____
_____
_____
_____

I am Thankful for:

_____
_____
_____
_____
_____

My Prayers for Others:
_____
_____
_____
_____
_____
_____
_____
_____

Notes and Reflections:
_____
_____
_____
_____
_____
_____
_____
_____
_____
_____
_____
_____
_____
_____
_____
_____
_____

Prayer Journal

Date:

Today's Passage:

_____

Prayer:

_____
_____
_____
_____

Devotional:

_____
_____
_____
_____

My Prayers that were Answered:

_____
_____
_____
_____

I am Thankful for:

_____
_____
_____
_____

My Prayers for Others:
_____
_____
_____
_____
_____
_____
_____
_____

Notes and Reflections:
_____
_____
_____
_____
_____
_____
_____
_____
_____
_____
_____
_____
_____
_____
_____
_____
_____
_____
_____

Prayer Journal

Date:

Today's Passage:

_____

Prayer:
_____
_____
_____
_____
_____

Devotional:
_____
_____
_____
_____
_____

My Prayers that were Answered:
_____
_____
_____
_____
_____

I am Thankful for:
_____
_____
_____
_____
_____

My Prayers for Others:

_____
_____
_____
_____
_____
_____
_____

Notes and Reflections:

_____
_____
_____
_____
_____
_____
_____
_____
_____
_____
_____
_____
_____
_____
_____
_____

Prayer Journal

Date:

Today's Passage:

_____

Prayer:

_____
_____
_____
_____

Devotional:

_____
_____
_____
_____

My Prayers that were Answered:

_____
_____
_____
_____

I am Thankful for:

_____
_____
_____
_____

My Prayers for Others:

_____
_____
_____
_____
_____
_____
_____
_____

Notes and Reflections:

_____
_____
_____
_____
_____
_____
_____
_____
_____
_____
_____
_____
_____
_____
_____
_____
_____
_____

Prayer Journal

Date:

Today's Passage:

_____

Prayer:
_____
_____
_____
_____

Devotional:
_____
_____
_____
_____

My Prayers that were Answered:
_____
_____
_____
_____

I am Thankful for:
_____
_____
_____
_____

My Prayers for Others:

_____
_____
_____
_____
_____
_____
_____

Notes and Reflections:

_____
_____
_____
_____
_____
_____
_____
_____
_____
_____
_____
_____
_____
_____
_____
_____
_____

Prayer Journal

Date:

Today's Passage:

_____

Prayer:

_____
_____
_____
_____

Devotional:

_____
_____
_____
_____

My Prayers that were Answered:

_____
_____
_____
_____

I am Thankful for:

_____
_____
_____
_____

My Prayers for Others:

_____
_____
_____
_____
_____
_____
_____
_____

Notes and Reflections:

_____
_____
_____
_____
_____
_____
_____
_____
_____
_____
_____
_____
_____
_____
_____
_____
_____

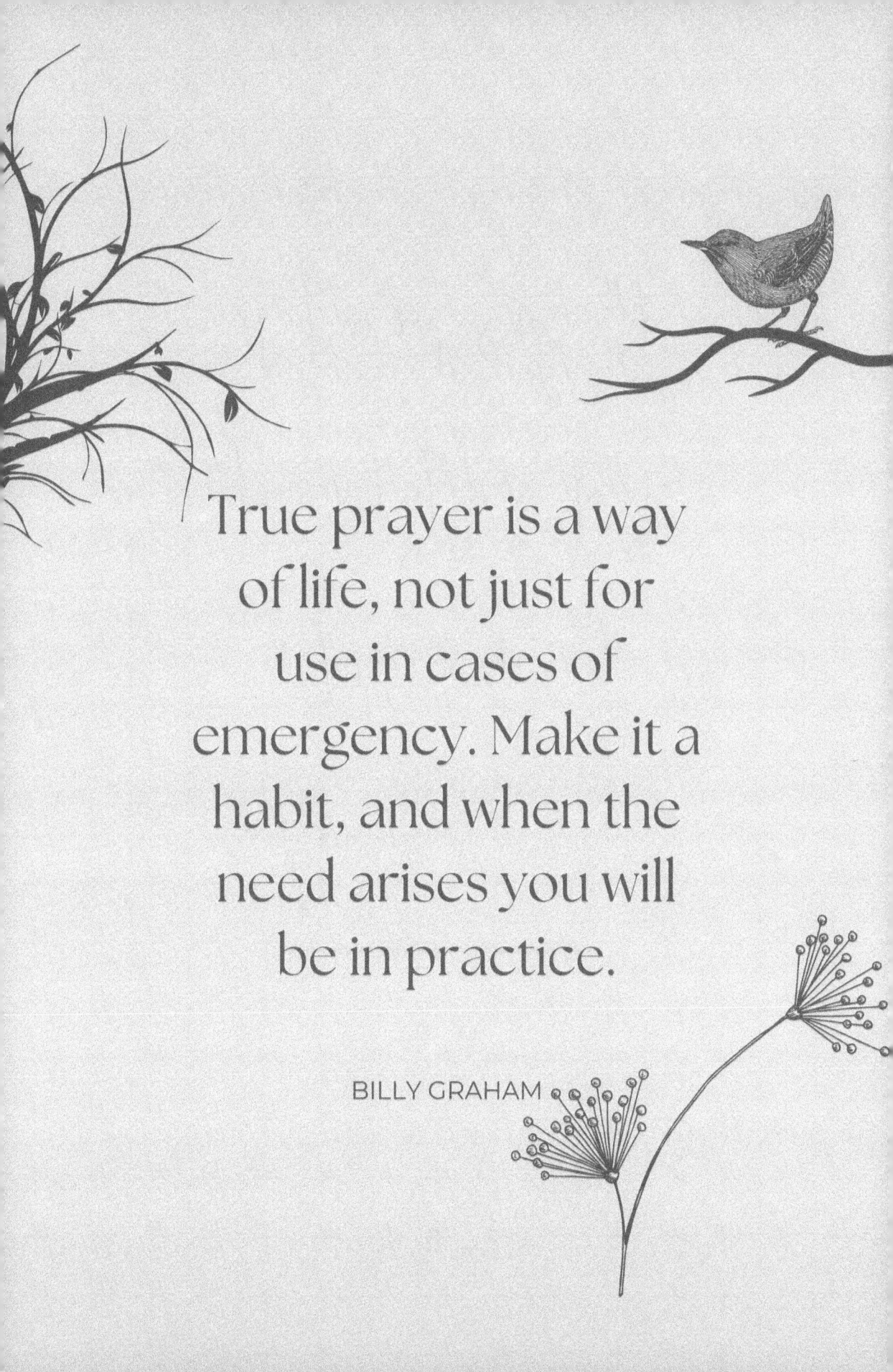

True prayer is a way of life, not just for use in cases of emergency. Make it a habit, and when the need arises you will be in practice.

BILLY GRAHAM

He gives power to the faint, and to him who has no might he increases strength.

———

Isaiah 40:29

Prayer Journal

Date:

Today's Passage:

_____

Prayer:
_____
_____
_____
_____
_____

Devotional:
_____
_____
_____
_____
_____

My Prayers that were Answered:
_____
_____
_____
_____
_____

I am Thankful for:
_____
_____
_____
_____
_____

My Prayers for Others:

_____
_____
_____
_____
_____
_____
_____
_____

Notes and Reflections:

_____
_____
_____
_____
_____
_____
_____
_____
_____
_____
_____
_____
_____
_____
_____
_____
_____
_____

Prayer Journal

Date:

Today's Passage:

_____

Prayer:
_____
_____
_____
_____
_____

Devotional:
_____
_____
_____
_____

My Prayers that were Answered:
_____
_____
_____
_____

I am Thankful for:
_____
_____
_____
_____

My Prayers for Others:

_____
_____
_____
_____
_____
_____
_____
_____

Notes and Reflections:

_____
_____
_____
_____
_____
_____
_____
_____
_____
_____
_____
_____
_____
_____
_____
_____
_____

Prayer Journal

Date:

Today's Passage:

_____

Prayer:
_____
_____
_____
_____
_____

Devotional:
_____
_____
_____
_____
_____

My Prayers that were Answered:
_____
_____
_____
_____
_____

I am Thankful for:
_____
_____
_____
_____
_____

My Prayers for Others:

_____
_____
_____
_____
_____
_____
_____
_____
_____

Notes and Reflections:

_____
_____
_____
_____
_____
_____
_____
_____
_____
_____
_____
_____
_____
_____
_____
_____
_____
_____

Prayer Journal

Date:

Today's Passage:

Prayer:
_____
_____
_____
_____

Devotional:
_____
_____
_____
_____

My Prayers that were Answered:
_____
_____
_____
_____

I am Thankful for:
_____
_____
_____
_____

My Prayers for Others:

_____
_____
_____
_____
_____
_____
_____

Notes and Reflections:

_____
_____
_____
_____
_____
_____
_____
_____
_____
_____
_____
_____
_____
_____
_____
_____
_____

Prayer Journal

Date:

Today's Passage:

_____

Prayer:
_____
_____
_____
_____
_____

Devotional:
_____
_____
_____
_____
_____

My Prayers that were Answered:
_____
_____
_____
_____
_____

I am Thankful for:
_____
_____
_____
_____
_____

My Prayers for Others:

_____
_____
_____
_____
_____
_____
_____
_____

Notes and Reflections:

_____
_____
_____
_____
_____
_____
_____
_____
_____
_____
_____
_____
_____
_____
_____
_____
_____
_____

Prayer Journal

Date:

Today's Passage:

_____

Prayer:
_____
_____
_____
_____
_____

Devotional:
_____
_____
_____
_____
_____

My Prayers that were Answered:
_____
_____
_____
_____
_____

I am Thankful for:
_____
_____
_____
_____
_____

My Prayers for Others:
___

Notes and Reflections:
___

Prayer Journal

Date:

Today's Passage:

_____

Prayer:
_____
_____
_____
_____
_____

Devotional:
_____
_____
_____
_____
_____

My Prayers that were Answered:
_____
_____
_____
_____
_____

I am Thankful for:
_____
_____
_____
_____
_____

My Prayers for Others:

_____
_____
_____
_____
_____
_____
_____
_____

Notes and Reflections:

_____
_____
_____
_____
_____
_____
_____
_____
_____
_____
_____
_____
_____
_____
_____
_____
_____
_____

Prayer Journal

Date:

Today's Passage:

_____

Prayer:
_____
_____
_____
_____

Devotional:
_____
_____
_____
_____

My Prayers that were Answered:
_____
_____
_____
_____

I am Thankful for:
_____
_____
_____
_____

My Prayers for Others:

___

Notes and Reflections:

___

Prayer Journal

Date:

Today's Passage:

_____

Prayer:
_____
_____
_____
_____
_____

Devotional:
_____
_____
_____
_____
_____

My Prayers that were Answered:
_____
_____
_____
_____
_____

I am Thankful for:
_____
_____
_____
_____
_____

My Prayers for Others:

_____
_____
_____
_____
_____
_____
_____
_____

Notes and Reflections:

_____
_____
_____
_____
_____
_____
_____
_____
_____
_____
_____
_____
_____
_____
_____
_____
_____
_____
_____

> If your day is hemmed in with prayer, it is less likely to come unraveled.
>
> CYNTHIA LEWIS

Be strong, and let your heart take courage, all you who wait for the Lord!

———

Psalm 31:24

Prayer Journal

Date:

Today's Passage:

_____

Prayer:
_____
_____
_____
_____
_____

Devotional:
_____
_____
_____
_____
_____

My Prayers that were Answered:
_____
_____
_____
_____

I am Thankful for:
_____
_____
_____
_____

My Prayers for Others:

_____
_____
_____
_____
_____
_____
_____
_____

Notes and Reflections:

_____
_____
_____
_____
_____
_____
_____
_____
_____
_____
_____
_____
_____
_____
_____
_____
_____
_____
_____

Prayer Journal

Date:

Today's Passage:

_____

Prayer:

_____
_____
_____
_____

Devotional:

_____
_____
_____
_____

My Prayers that were Answered:

_____
_____
_____
_____

I am Thankful for:

_____
_____
_____
_____

My Prayers for Others:

___

Notes and Reflections:

___

Prayer Journal

Date:

Today's Passage:

Prayer:
_____
_____
_____
_____

Devotional:
_____
_____
_____
_____

My Prayers that were Answered:
_____
_____
_____
_____

I am Thankful for:
_____
_____
_____
_____

My Prayers for Others:

_____
_____
_____
_____
_____
_____
_____
_____

Notes and Reflections:

_____
_____
_____
_____
_____
_____
_____
_____
_____
_____
_____
_____
_____
_____
_____
_____
_____
_____

Prayer Journal

Date:

Today's Passage:

_____

Prayer:
_____
_____
_____
_____
_____

Devotional:
_____
_____
_____
_____
_____

My Prayers that were Answered:
_____
_____
_____
_____
_____

I am Thankful for:
_____
_____
_____
_____
_____

My Prayers for Others:

___

Notes and Reflections:

___

Prayer Journal

Date:

Today's Passage:

_____

Prayer:
_____
_____
_____
_____
_____

Devotional:
_____
_____
_____
_____

My Prayers that were Answered:
_____
_____
_____
_____

I am Thankful for:
_____
_____
_____
_____

My Prayers for Others:

_____
_____
_____
_____
_____
_____
_____

Notes and Reflections:

_____
_____
_____
_____
_____
_____
_____
_____
_____
_____
_____
_____
_____
_____
_____
_____
_____
_____

Prayer Journal

Date:

Today's Passage:

_____

Prayer:
_____
_____
_____
_____
_____

Devotional:
_____
_____
_____
_____
_____

My Prayers that were Answered:
_____
_____
_____
_____
_____

I am Thankful for:
_____
_____
_____
_____
_____

My Prayers for Others:

_____
_____
_____
_____
_____
_____
_____

Notes and Reflections:

_____
_____
_____
_____
_____
_____
_____
_____
_____
_____
_____
_____
_____
_____
_____
_____
_____
_____

Prayer Journal

Date:

Today's Passage:

_____

Prayer:
_____
_____
_____
_____

Devotional:
_____
_____
_____
_____

My Prayers that were Answered:
_____
_____
_____
_____

I am Thankful for:
_____
_____
_____
_____

My Prayers for Others:
_____
_____
_____
_____
_____
_____
_____
_____

Notes and Reflections:
_____
_____
_____
_____
_____
_____
_____
_____
_____
_____
_____
_____
_____
_____
_____
_____
_____

Prayer Journal

Date:

Today's Passage:

_____

Prayer:
_____
_____
_____
_____
_____

Devotional:
_____
_____
_____
_____
_____

My Prayers that were Answered:
_____
_____
_____
_____
_____

I am Thankful for:
_____
_____
_____
_____
_____

My Prayers for Others:

_____
_____
_____
_____
_____
_____
_____
_____

Notes and Reflections:

_____
_____
_____
_____
_____
_____
_____
_____
_____
_____
_____
_____
_____
_____
_____
_____
_____

Prayer Journal

Date:

Today's Passage:

_____

Prayer:
_____
_____
_____
_____

Devotional:
_____
_____
_____
_____

My Prayers that were Answered:
_____
_____
_____
_____

I am Thankful for:
_____
_____
_____
_____

My Prayers for Others:

_____
_____
_____
_____
_____
_____
_____
_____

Notes and Reflections:

_____
_____
_____
_____
_____
_____
_____
_____
_____
_____
_____
_____
_____
_____
_____
_____
_____

God shapes the world by prayer. The more praying there is in the world the better the world will be, the mightier the forces against evil.

MOTHER TERESA

God is our refuge and strength, a very present help in trouble.

Psalm 46:1

Prayer Journal

Date:

Today's Passage:

_____

Prayer:
_____
_____
_____
_____

Devotional:
_____
_____
_____
_____

My Prayers that were Answered:
_____
_____
_____
_____

I am Thankful for:
_____
_____
_____
_____

My Prayers for Others:
_____
_____
_____
_____
_____
_____
_____
_____

Notes and Reflections:
_____
_____
_____
_____
_____
_____
_____
_____
_____
_____
_____
_____
_____
_____
_____
_____
_____
_____

Prayer Journal

Date:

Today's Passage:

_____

Prayer:
_____
_____
_____
_____
_____

Devotional:
_____
_____
_____
_____
_____

My Prayers that were Answered:
_____
_____
_____
_____

I am Thankful for:
_____
_____
_____
_____

My Prayers for Others:
_____
_____
_____
_____
_____
_____
_____
_____

Notes and Reflections:
_____
_____
_____
_____
_____
_____
_____
_____
_____
_____
_____
_____
_____
_____
_____
_____
_____

Prayer Journal

Date:

Today's Passage:

_____

Prayer:
_____
_____
_____
_____

Devotional:
_____
_____
_____
_____

My Prayers that were Answered:
_____
_____
_____
_____

I am Thankful for:
_____
_____
_____
_____

My Prayers for Others:

_____
_____
_____
_____
_____
_____
_____
_____

Notes and Reflections:

_____
_____
_____
_____
_____
_____
_____
_____
_____
_____
_____
_____
_____
_____
_____
_____
_____

Prayer Journal

Date:

Today's Passage:

_____

Prayer:
_____
_____
_____
_____
_____

Devotional:
_____
_____
_____
_____
_____

My Prayers that were Answered:
_____
_____
_____
_____
_____

I am Thankful for:
_____
_____
_____
_____
_____

My Prayers for Others:

___

Notes and Reflections:

___

Prayer Journal

Date:

Today's Passage:

_____

Prayer:
_____
_____
_____
_____
_____

Devotional:
_____
_____
_____
_____
_____

My Prayers that were Answered:
_____
_____
_____
_____
_____

I am Thankful for:
_____
_____
_____
_____
_____

My Prayers for Others:

_____
_____
_____
_____
_____
_____
_____
_____

Notes and Reflections:

_____
_____
_____
_____
_____
_____
_____
_____
_____
_____
_____
_____
_____
_____
_____
_____
_____

Prayer Journal

Date:

Today's Passage:

_____

Prayer:
_____
_____
_____
_____
_____

Devotional:
_____
_____
_____
_____
_____

My Prayers that were Answered:
_____
_____
_____
_____
_____

I am Thankful for:
_____
_____
_____
_____
_____

My Prayers for Others:

_____
_____
_____
_____
_____
_____
_____
_____

Notes and Reflections:

_____
_____
_____
_____
_____
_____
_____
_____
_____
_____
_____
_____
_____
_____
_____
_____
_____
_____
_____
_____

Prayer Journal

Date:

Today's Passage:

_____

Prayer:
_____
_____
_____
_____

Devotional:
_____
_____
_____
_____

My Prayers that were Answered:
_____
_____
_____
_____

I am Thankful for:
_____
_____
_____
_____

My Prayers for Others:
___

Notes and Reflections:
___

Prayer Journal

Date:

Today's Passage:

_____

Prayer:
_____
_____
_____
_____
_____

Devotional:
_____
_____
_____
_____
_____

My Prayers that were Answered:
_____
_____
_____
_____
_____

I am Thankful for:
_____
_____
_____
_____
_____

My Prayers for Others:

___

Notes and Reflections:

___

Prayer Journal

Date:

Today's Passage:

_____

Prayer:
_____
_____
_____
_____

Devotional:
_____
_____
_____
_____

My Prayers that were Answered:
_____
_____
_____
_____

I am Thankful for:
_____
_____
_____
_____

My Prayers for Others:

_____
_____
_____
_____
_____
_____
_____
_____

Notes and Reflections:

_____
_____
_____
_____
_____
_____
_____
_____
_____
_____
_____
_____
_____
_____
_____
_____
_____
_____

Prayer Journal

Date:

Today's Passage:

_____

Prayer:
_____
_____
_____
_____
_____

Devotional:
_____
_____
_____
_____
_____

My Prayers that were Answered:
_____
_____
_____
_____
_____

I am Thankful for:
_____
_____
_____
_____
_____

My Prayers for Others:
_____
_____
_____
_____
_____
_____
_____
_____

Notes and Reflections:
_____
_____
_____
_____
_____
_____
_____
_____
_____
_____
_____
_____
_____
_____
_____
_____
_____

Prayer Journal

Date:

Today's Passage:

_____

Prayer:
_____
_____
_____
_____

Devotional:
_____
_____
_____
_____

My Prayers that were Answered:
_____
_____
_____
_____

I am Thankful for:
_____
_____
_____
_____

My Prayers for Others:

_____
_____
_____
_____
_____
_____
_____

Notes and Reflections:

_____
_____
_____
_____
_____
_____
_____
_____
_____
_____
_____
_____
_____
_____
_____
_____

Prayer Journal

Date:

Today's Passage:

_____

Prayer:
_____
_____
_____
_____

Devotional:
_____
_____
_____
_____

My Prayers that were Answered:
_____
_____
_____
_____

I am Thankful for:
_____
_____
_____
_____

My Prayers for Others:

___

Notes and Reflections:

___

Prayer Journal

Date:

Today's Passage:

_____

Prayer:
_____
_____
_____
_____

Devotional:
_____
_____
_____
_____

My Prayers that were Answered:
_____
_____
_____
_____

I am Thankful for:
_____
_____
_____
_____

My Prayers for Others:
_____
_____
_____
_____
_____
_____
_____
_____
_____

Notes and Reflections:
_____
_____
_____
_____
_____
_____
_____
_____
_____
_____
_____
_____
_____
_____
_____
_____
_____

To get nations back on their feet, we must first get down on our knees.

BILLY GRAHAM

But seek first the kingdom of God and his righteousness, and all these things will be added to you.

———

Matthew 6:33

Prayer Journal

Date:

Today's Passage:

_____

Prayer:
_____
_____
_____
_____
_____

Devotional:
_____
_____
_____
_____
_____

My Prayers that were Answered:
_____
_____
_____
_____
_____

I am Thankful for:
_____
_____
_____
_____
_____

My Prayers for Others:

_____
_____
_____
_____
_____
_____
_____
_____

Notes and Reflections:

_____
_____
_____
_____
_____
_____
_____
_____
_____
_____
_____
_____
_____
_____
_____
_____
_____
_____
_____

Prayer Journal

Date:

Today's Passage:

_____

Prayer:
_____
_____
_____
_____
_____

Devotional:
_____
_____
_____
_____
_____

My Prayers that were Answered:
_____
_____
_____
_____
_____

I am Thankful for:
_____
_____
_____
_____
_____

My Prayers for Others:

_____
_____
_____
_____
_____
_____
_____

Notes and Reflections:

_____
_____
_____
_____
_____
_____
_____
_____
_____
_____
_____
_____
_____
_____
_____
_____
_____

Prayer Journal

Date:

Today's Passage:

_____

Prayer:
_____
_____
_____
_____

Devotional:
_____
_____
_____
_____

My Prayers that were Answered:
_____
_____
_____
_____

I am Thankful for:
_____
_____
_____
_____

My Prayers for Others:

_____
_____
_____
_____
_____
_____
_____
_____

Notes and Reflections:

_____
_____
_____
_____
_____
_____
_____
_____
_____
_____
_____
_____
_____
_____
_____
_____
_____

Prayer Journal

Date:

Today's Passage:

_____

Prayer:

_____
_____
_____
_____

Devotional:

_____
_____
_____
_____

My Prayers that were Answered:

_____
_____
_____
_____

I am Thankful for:

_____
_____
_____
_____

My Prayers for Others:

_____
_____
_____
_____
_____
_____
_____

Notes and Reflections:

_____
_____
_____
_____
_____
_____
_____
_____
_____
_____
_____
_____
_____
_____
_____
_____
_____

Prayer Journal

Date:

Today's Passage:

_____

Prayer:
_____
_____
_____
_____

Devotional:
_____
_____
_____
_____

My Prayers that were Answered:
_____
_____
_____
_____

I am Thankful for:
_____
_____
_____
_____

My Prayers for Others:

_____
_____
_____
_____
_____
_____
_____
_____

Notes and Reflections:

_____
_____
_____
_____
_____
_____
_____
_____
_____
_____
_____
_____
_____
_____
_____
_____
_____
_____

Prayer Journal

Date:

Today's Passage:

_____

Prayer:

_____
_____
_____
_____
_____

Devotional:

_____
_____
_____
_____
_____

My Prayers that were Answered:

_____
_____
_____
_____
_____

I am Thankful for:

_____
_____
_____
_____
_____

My Prayers for Others:

_____
_____
_____
_____
_____
_____
_____

Notes and Reflections:

_____
_____
_____
_____
_____
_____
_____
_____
_____
_____
_____
_____
_____
_____
_____
_____

Prayer should not be regarded as a duty which must be performed, but rather as a privilege to be enjoyed, a rare delight that is always revealing some new beauty.

E M BOUNDS

For nothing will be impossible with God.

———————

Luke 1:37

Prayer Journal

Date:

Today's Passage:

_____

Prayer:
_____
_____
_____
_____

Devotional:
_____
_____
_____
_____

My Prayers that were Answered:
_____
_____
_____
_____

I am Thankful for:
_____
_____
_____
_____

My Prayers for Others:

_____
_____
_____
_____
_____
_____
_____
_____

Notes and Reflections:

_____
_____
_____
_____
_____
_____
_____
_____
_____
_____
_____
_____
_____
_____
_____
_____
_____
_____

Prayer Journal

Date:

Today's Passage:

_____

Prayer:
_____
_____
_____
_____

Devotional:
_____
_____
_____
_____

My Prayers that were Answered:
_____
_____
_____
_____

I am Thankful for:
_____
_____
_____
_____

My Prayers for Others:

_____
_____
_____
_____
_____
_____
_____
_____

Notes and Reflections:

_____
_____
_____
_____
_____
_____
_____
_____
_____
_____
_____
_____
_____
_____
_____
_____

More info on Roma:

www.romawaterman.com

www.training.romawaterman.com

———————

www.ingramcontent.com/pod-product-compliance
Lightning Source LLC
Chambersburg PA
CBHW061138010526
44107CB00069B/2977